Annie's

Baby Bright Quilts

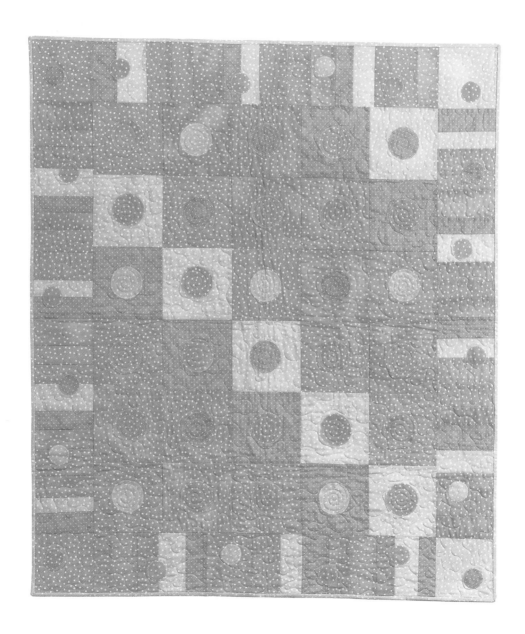

LEISURE ARTS, INC. • Maumelle, Arkansas

This book will become your go-to source when a special baby quilt is needed. You'll find perfect projects for shower gifts, or maybe you're looking for a quilt for that special toddler in your life. Simply pick your pattern, select your fabrics, and start stitching. There are 10 lovely and inspiring baby quilts just waiting for you to put your personal spin on them.

ENJOY!

ANNIE'S STAFF
EDITOR **Carolyn S. Vagts**
CREATIVE DIRECTOR **Brad Snow**
PUBLISHING SERVICES DIRECTOR **Brenda Gallmeyer**
MANAGING EDITOR **Barb Sprunger**
TECHNICAL EDITORS **Angie Buckles, Sandra L. Hatch**
COPY MANAGER **Corene Painter**
SENIOR COPY EDITOR **Emily Carter**
TECHNICAL ARTISTS **Connie Rand, Debera Kuntz**
SENIOR PRODUCTION ARTIST **Nicole Gage**
PRODUCTION ARTISTS **Glenda Chamberlain, Edith Teegarden**
PRODUCTION ASSISTANTS **Laurie Lehman, Marj Morgan, Judy Neuenschwander**
PHOTOGRAPHY SUPERVISOR **Tammy Christian**
PHOTOGRAPHY **Matthew Owen**
PHOTO STYLISTS **Tammy Liechty, Tammy Steiner**

CHIEF EXECUTIVE OFFICER **David McKee**
EXECUTIVE VICE PRESIDENT **Michele Fortune**

LEISURE ARTS STAFF
Editorial Staff
CREATIVE ART DIRECTOR **Katherine Laughlin**
PUBLICATIONS DIRECTOR **Leah Lampirez**
SPECIAL PROJECTS DIRECTOR **Susan Frantz Wiles**
PREPRESS TECHNICIAN **Stephanie Johnson**

Business Staff
PRESIDENT AND CHIEF EXECUTIVE OFFICER **Fred F. Pruss**
SENIOR VICE PRESIDENT OF OPERATIONS **Jim Dittrich**
VICE PRESIDENT OF RETAIL SALES **Martha Adams**
CHIEF FINANCIAL OFFICER **Tiffany P. Childers**
CONTROLLER **Teresa Eby**
INFORMATION TECHNOLOGY DIRECTOR **Brian Roden**
DIRECTOR OF E-COMMERCE **Mark Hawkins**
MANAGER OF E-COMMERCE **Robert Young**

ISBN-13/EAN: 978-1-4647-3334-5
UPC: 0-28906-06441-4

PROJECTS

11

13

39

31

19

Color Therapy Throw

Simple Nine-Patch blocks, each constructed in a different color with white in the center, will give you endless options for layout. Add some appliqué, and you have a treasure.

Design by Chris Malone

Skill Level
Intermediate

Finished Size
Throw Size: 57½" x 57½"
Block Size: 7½" x 7½" Finished
Number of Blocks: 25

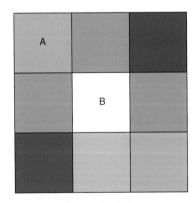

Nine-Patch
7½" x 7½" Finished Block
Make 25

CUTTING

Prepare appliqué templates using patterns provided and referring to Quilting Basics on page 46. Cut appliqué pieces per pattern and instructions.

From each assorted yellow, orange, red, pink, blue, turquoise and leaf green scraps:
* Cut 24 (3") A squares to total 168.

From assorted purple and green scraps:
* Cut 16 (3") A squares each to total 32 additional A squares.

From assorted scraps:
* Cut 16 (1½") C squares total.

From green dot:
* Cut 1⅝"-wide bias strips to total 4 (24") strips when joined for vines.

From white tonal:
* Cut 2 (8½" x 42") E strips.
* Cut 2 (8½" x 58") F strips along fabric length.
* Cut 3 (3" by remaining fabric width) strips. Subcut strips into 24 (3") B squares.
* Cut 3 (8" by remaining fabric width) strips. Subcut strips into 40 (1½" x 8") D sashing strips and 1 (3") B square to total 25 B squares.

COMPLETING THE NINE-PATCH BLOCKS

1. Select one B square and eight A squares from one color family.
2. Arrange and join the A and B squares in rows referring to Figure 1; press.

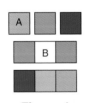

Figure 1

Appliqué Tip

Use pinking shears to cut out the stitched fabric/interfacing circles and eliminate the need to clip into seams to allow them to stretch enough to make smooth finished edges.

---

3. Join the rows to complete one Nine-Patch block referring to Figure 2; press.

Figure 2

4. Repeat steps 1–3 to make a total of 25 Nine-Patch blocks.

COMPLETING THE PIECED TOP

1. Arrange and join five Nine-Patch blocks with four D strips to make a block row; press seams toward D. Repeat to make a total of five block rows.
2. Join five D strips with four C squares to make a sashing row; press seams toward D. Repeat to make a total of four sashing rows.
3. Join the sashing rows with the block rows to complete the pieced center; press seams toward sashing rows.
4. Sew E strips to the top and bottom, and F strips to opposite sides of the pieced center; press seams toward strips.

COMPLETING THE APPLIQUÉ

1. Join green dot bias strips as necessary to make four 1⅝" x 24" strips.
2. Fold each bias strip in half wrong sides together along the length and stitch with a scant ¼" seam; trim seam to ⅛".
3. Insert bias pressing bar inside one stitched bias strip and press with seam centered on one side to make a vine strip referring to Figure 3. Repeat with each strip to make a total of four vine strips.

Figure 3

4. In bottom right corner, starting 9¼" in from right side and 3" up from the bottom, pin and stitch one vine strip in a gentle curve along the E border strip as shown in Figure 4.

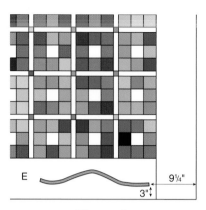

Figure 4

5. Repeat step 4 with a second vine strip starting 10¼" up from the bottom and 3" in from the right side, referring to Figure 5.

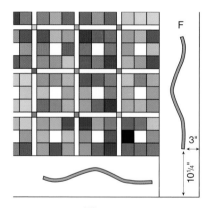

Figure 5

6. Repeat steps 4 and 5 with a second set of vine strips on the top left corner of the pieced center.
7. To prepare circle flowers, use a compass to draw circle shapes on the template material in the following sizes: 1¼", 1½", 2½", 3½" and 5". Cut out templates on drawn lines.
8. Choose fabric scraps for flower centers and flowers. Using prepared templates, trace the following sizes onto the wrong sides of the chosen scraps (do not cut out): two 5" flowers with two each 1¼" and 2½" centers, 10 (3½") flowers with 10 (1½" centers), and four 2½" flowers with four 1¼" centers.

9. Pin a marked scrap piece right sides together with the lightweight interfacing and stitch on the traced circle line all around as shown in Figure 6.

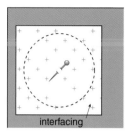

interfacing

Figure 6

10. Cut out circle close to, but not through, the stitching line using pinking shears.
11. Repeat steps 9 and 10 with remaining traced circles.
12. Cut a slash in the interfacing side only and turn each circle right side out through the slash; press edges smooth and flat.
13. Pin the flower centers to the flowers referring to step 8 for size combinations; hand-stitch in place.
14. Prepare 20 leaf shapes in the same manner as for flowers using pattern provided.
15. Arrange and hand-stitch the flowers and leaf shapes on the previously stitched vine strips to complete the throw top as shown in Figure 7.

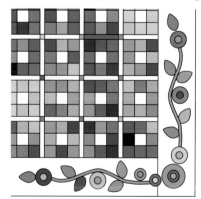

Figure 7

Appliqué Tip

Although some quilters prefer to remove excess fabric from behind large appliqué pieces, the extra layers will create a slight dimension, especially with the interfacing method of appliqué. Cutting out sections of the background can also weaken the integrity of the quilt.

COMPLETING THE THROW

1. Sandwich the batting between the pieced top and a prepared backing piece; pin or baste layers together to hold. Quilt flower shapes and centers of blocks using larger quilting stitches and pearl cotton in various colors to match blocks or scraps. Quilt vein lines in leaves referring to leaf pattern.

2. When quilting is complete, trim batting and backing fabric even with raw edges of the pieced top.

3. Join binding strips on the short ends to make a 250"-long strip; press seams open. Fold the binding strip with wrong sides together along length; press.

4. Sew binding to the edges, mitering corners and overlapping ends. Fold binding to the back side and stitch in place to finish. ●

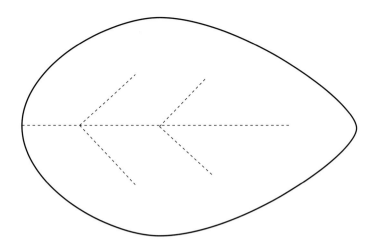

Color Therapy Throw
Leaf
Make a total of 20 green & leaf green scraps
as per instructions

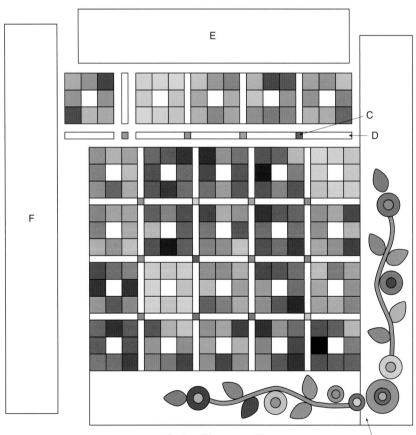

Color Therapy Throw
Assembly Diagram 57½" x 57½"

Also add appliqué as shown
here to upper right corner.

Appliqué Tip

The appliqué shapes may be machine-stitched using a blanket stitch, satin stitch or zigzag stitch instead of being hand-stitched. If using this method, except for one small flower that overlaps both E and F borders, stitch the vines and flowers on the border strips before stitching them to the pieced center. The final flowers may be machine-stitched in place after the borders have been stitched. This eliminates the need to have the entire quilt at the machine for the appliqué process during the bulk of the machine work.

Color Therapy Throw Alternate Size
Assembly Diagram 66" x 91½"
Make 54 blocks and join in 9 rows of 6 blocks each to make
a twin-size quilt. Remember to purchase more fabric for
borders, sashing and binding.

Also add appliqué as shown
here to upper right corner.

Twist & Turn

A quilter can make this quilt quickly using precut triangles. You can start in the morning and be finished that evening. For a different look, try mixing blacks and whites, or stripes and a single solid color.

Design by Cathy Lee

Skill Level
Intermediate

Finished Size
Quilt Size: 40" x 48½"
Block Size: 8½" x 8½" Finished
Number of Blocks: 20

MATERIALS

- 80 coordinating precut 6" x 6" triangles (A)
- ⅓ yard aqua solid
- ¾ yard bubblegum pink solid
- ⅞ yard yellow solid
- Batting to size
- Backing to size
- Thread
- Spray starch or fabric stabilizer (optional)
- Basic sewing tools and supplies

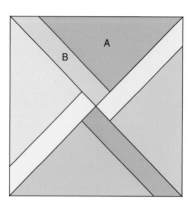

Twist & Turn
8½" x 8½" Finished Block
Make 20

CUTTING

From aqua solid, bubblegum pink solid and yellow solid:
- Cut 1 (8" by fabric width) strip each fabric. Subcut 28 (1½" x 8") B strips each fabric. *Note: You will have 4 extra B strips.*

From bubblegum pink solid:
- Cut 5 (2¼" by fabric width) binding strips.

From yellow solid:
- Cut 3 (3½" by fabric width) strips. Join on short ends to make one long strip; press seams open. Subcut strips into 2 (3½" x 43") C strips.
- Cut 2 (3½" x 40½") D strips.

COMPLETING THE BLOCKS

1. To make one Twist & Turn block, select four A triangles and four B strips of any color.
2. Align one end of one B strip with square end of one A triangle and stitch to make an A-B unit as shown in Figure 1; press seam toward A.

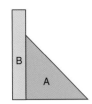

Figure 1

3. Repeat step 2 with the remaining three A and B pieces, sewing B to the same side of each triangle.
4. Join two A-B units as shown in Figure 2; press seam to one side. Repeat to make two units.

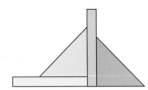

Figure 2

5. Join the two units as shown in Figure 3; press seam in one direction.

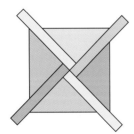

Figure 3

6. Using a ruler and rotary cutter, trim excess B and square up to 9" x 9" to complete one Twist & Turn block.
7. Repeat steps 1–6 to complete a total of 20 Twist & Turn blocks. **Note:** *All edges of these blocks will be bias edges. To prevent stretching when stitching, apply spray starch or fabric stabilizer.*

COMPLETING THE QUILT

1. Arrange and join four Twist & Turn blocks to make a row; press seams in one direction. Repeat to make five rows, pressing seams in adjoining rows in opposite directions.
2. Join the rows to complete the pieced center; press seams in one direction.
3. Sew a C strip to opposite long sides and D strips to the top and bottom of the pieced center to complete the quilt top; press seams toward strips.
4. Create a quilt sandwich referring to Quilting Basics on page 46.
5. Quilt as desired.
6. Bind referring to Quilting Basics on page 46 to finish. ●

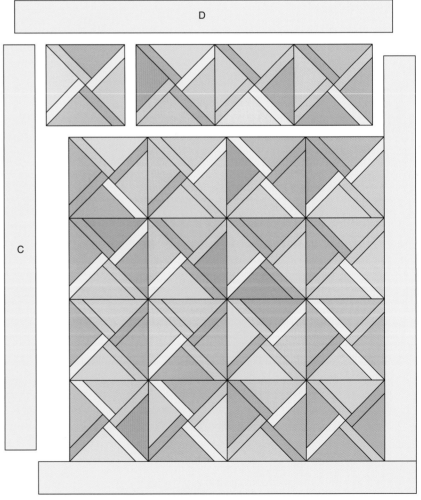

Twist & Turn
Assembly Diagram 40" x 48½"

Nite-Time Baby Bear

Appliquéd teddy bears make the perfect quilt for Baby.

Design by Rochelle Martin for Cottage Quilt Designs

Skill Level
Beginner

Finished Size
Quilt Size: 46" x 62"
Block Sizes: 8" x 8" Finished and 16" x 16" Finished
Number of Blocks: 20 and 1

MATERIALS

- ⅛ yard blue duck print
- ⅛ yard tan tonal
- ⅛ yard black solid
- ⅜ yard brown print
- ⅔ yard yellow print
- 1½ yards cream print
- 1⅛ yards white print
- 1½ yards blue ring print
- Backing to size
- Batting to size
- Thread
- 1⅛ yards 12"-wide fusible web
- 1 yard fabric stabilizer
- Basic sewing tools and supplies

Large Baby Bear
16" x 16" Finished Block
Make 1

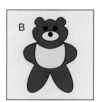

Small Baby Bear
8" x 8" Finished Block
Make 4

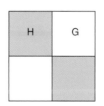

Four-Patch
8" x 8" Finished Block
Make 4

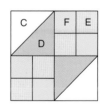

Jacob's Ladder
8" x 8" Finished Block
Make 12

CUTTING

Prepare appliqué templates referring to Quilting Basics on page 46 and using patterns provided. Cut as instructed on patterns and in instructions.

From yellow print:
- Cut 3 (2½" x 42") F strips.
- Cut 3 (2½" x 42") I strips.
- Cut 2 (2½" x 36½") J strips.

From cream print:
- Cut 1 (16½" x 42") strip.
  Subcut 1 (16½") A square.
- Cut 1 (8½" x 42") strip.
  Subcut 4 (8½") B squares.
- Cut 3 (2½" x 42") E strips.

From white print:
- Cut 2 (4⅞" x 42") strips.
  Subcut 12 (4⅞") squares. Cut each square in half on 1 diagonal to make 24 C triangles.
- Cut 1 (4½" x 42") G strip.
- Cut 3 (2½" x 42") K strips.
- Cut 2 (2½" x 40½") L strips.

From blue ring print:
- Cut 2 (4⅞" x 42") strips.
  Subcut 12 (4⅞") squares. Cut each square in half on 1 diagonal to make 24 D triangles.
- Cut 1 (4½" x 42") H strip.
- Cut 5 (3½" x 42") M/N strips.
- Cut (2¼" x 42") binding strips.

COMPLETING THE JACOB'S LADDER BLOCKS

1. Sew an E strip to an F strip with right sides together along length; press seams toward F strips. Repeat to make three E-F strip sets.

2. Subcut the E-F strip set into 48 (2½") E-F units as shown in Figure 1.

Figure 1

3. Join two E-F units to make a Four-Patch unit as shown in Figure 2; press seam in one direction. Repeat to make 24 Four-Patch units.

Figure 2   **Figure 3**

4. Sew C to D along the diagonal to make a C-D unit as shown in Figure 3; press seam toward D. Repeat to make 24 C-D units.

Nite-Time Baby Bear
Assembly Diagram 46" x 62"

5. To complete one Jacob's Ladder block, join one each Four-Patch unit and C-D unit to make a row as shown in Figure 4; press seam toward the C-D unit. Repeat to make two rows.

Figure 4

6. Join the rows referring to the block drawing to complete one block; press seam in one direction.

7. Repeat steps 5 and 6 to complete 12 Jacob's Ladder blocks.

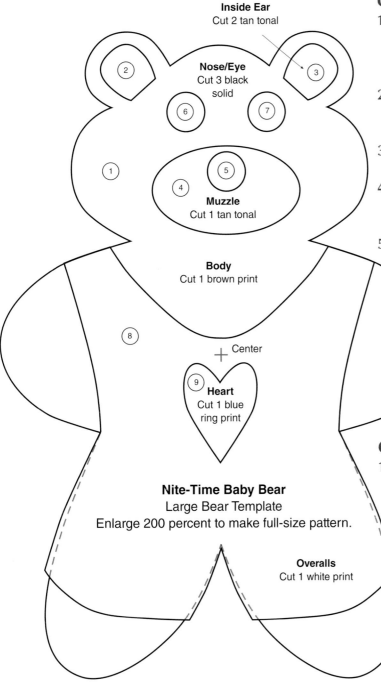

Inside Ear
Cut 2 tan tonal

Nose/Eye
Cut 3 black solid

Muzzle
Cut 1 tan tonal

Body
Cut 1 brown print

+ Center

Heart
Cut 1 blue ring print

Nite-Time Baby Bear
Large Bear Template
Enlarge 200 percent to make full-size pattern.

Overalls
Cut 1 white print

COMPLETING THE FOUR-PATCH BLOCKS

1. Sew the G strip to the H strip with right sides together along length; press seam toward H strip.

2. Subcut the G-H strip set into eight 4½" G-H units as shown in Figure 5.

Figure 5

3. Join two G-H units referring to the block drawing to complete one Four-Patch block; press seam in one direction. Repeat to make four blocks.

COMPLETING THE APPLIQUÉ BLOCKS

1. Trace appliqué shapes for the large and small bear motifs onto the paper side of the fusible web as directed on each piece; cut out shapes leaving a margin around each one.

2. Fuse shapes to the wrong side of fabrics as directed on patterns for color; cut out shapes on traced lines. Remove paper backing.

3. Fold and crease each A and B square to mark the vertical and horizontal centers.

4. Arrange and fuse the large bear shapes on A, matching the center of the piece to the creased center on A.

5. Repeat step 4 with small bear pieces on B squares to fuse four small bear motifs.

6. Cut one 16" and four 8" squares fabric stabilizer; pin a stabilizer square to the wrong side of the fused blocks.

7. Using thread to match fabrics and a machine buttonhole or blanket stitch, stitch around each shape. When stitching is complete, remove fabric stabilizer to complete the blocks.

COMPLETING THE QUILT

1. Join one each Small Baby Bear block with one Four-Patch block to make a Bear side row as shown in Figure 6; press seam toward Small Baby Bear block. Repeat to make four Bear side rows referring to the Assembly Diagram for positioning of blocks in each row.

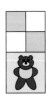

Figure 6

2. Join four Jacob's Ladder blocks to make a star unit as shown in Figure 7; press seams in opposite directions and then in one direction. Repeat to make two star units.

Figure 7

3. Sew a Bear row to opposite sides of each star unit to make the top and bottom rows referring to the Assembly Diagram for positioning; press seams toward Bear side rows.

4. Join two Jacob's Ladder blocks to make a side row as shown in Figure 8; press seam in one direction. Repeat to make two side rows.

Figure 8   **Figure 9**

5. Sew a side row to opposite sides of the Large Baby Bear block to complete the center row as shown in Figure 9; press seams away from the side rows.

6. Join the rows referring to the Assembly Diagram to complete the pieced center; press seams toward center row.

7. Join the I strips with right sides together on short ends to make one long strip; press seams open. Subcut strip into two 48½" I strips.

8. Sew an I strip to opposite long sides and J strips to the top and bottom of the pieced center; press seams toward I and J strips.

9. Join the K strips with right sides together on short ends to make one long strip; press seams open. Subcut strip into two 52½" K strips.

10. Sew a K strip to opposite long sides and L strips to the top and bottom of the pieced center; press seams toward K and L strips.

11. Join the M/N strips with right sides together on short ends to make one long strip; press seams open. Subcut strip into two 56½" M strips and two 46½" N strips.

12. Sew M strips to opposite long sides and N strips to the top and bottom of the pieced center to complete the pieced top; press seams toward M and N strips.

13. Create a quilt sandwich referring to Quilting Basics on page 46.

14. Quilt as desired.

15. Bind referring to Quilting Basics on page 46 to finish. ●

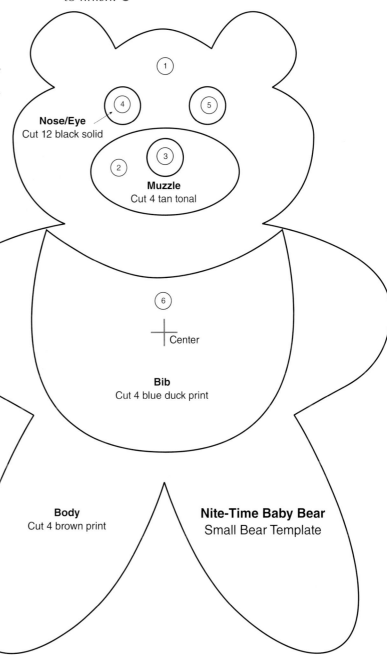

Nose/Eye
Cut 12 black solid

Muzzle
Cut 4 tan tonal

Center

Bib
Cut 4 blue duck print

Body
Cut 4 brown print

Nite-Time Baby Bear
Small Bear Template

It's Not Easy Being Green

A certain famous frog finds that it's not easy being green, but in this quilt, green is the perfect color.

Design by Carolyn S. Vagts for The Village Pattern Co.

Skill Level
Beginner

Finished Size
Quilt Size: 49" x 73"
Block Size: 12" x 12" Finished
Number of Blocks: 15

MATERIALS

- Scrap solid black
- ⅜ yard each 9 different aqua and blue tonals
- ⅓ yard yellow solid
- ½ yard green tonal
- ¾ yard light blue tonal
- 1⅛ yards medium blue tonal
- Backing to size
- Batting to size
- Thread
- 1 yard paper-backed fusible web
- Basic sewing tools and supplies

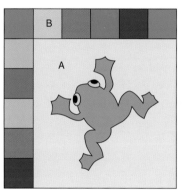

Frog
12" x 12" Finished Block
Make 8

Nine-Patch
12" x 12" Finished Block
Make 7

CUTTING

From aqua and blue tonals:
- Cut 1(2½" by fabric width) strip each.
  Subcut a total of 88 (2½") B squares.
- Cut 1 (4½" by fabric width) strip each.
  Subcut a total of 63 (4½") C squares.
- Cut 6 (2¼" by fabric width) binding strips.

From yellow solid:
- Cut 2(1½" x 36½") D strips.
- Cut 3 (1½" by fabric width) E strips.

From light blue tonal:
- Cut 2 (10½" by fabric width) rectangles. Subcut 8 (10½") A squares.

From medium blue tonal:
- Cut 2 (6" x 38½") F strips.
- Cut 4 (6" x 42") G strips.

COMPLETING THE FROG BLOCKS

1. Trace the frog motif onto the paper side of the fusible web as directed on patterns for number to cut; cut out shapes, leaving a margin around each one.
2. Fuse shapes to the wrong side of fabrics as directed; cut out shapes on traced lines. Remove paper backing.
3. Fold each A square in half vertically and horizontally, and crease to mark the centers.
4. Matching X on the frog motif to center of A, fuse the frog pieces on each A square in numerical order.
5. Straight-stitch around the edges of each fused shape using thread to match fabrics.
6. To complete one Frog block, join five B squares; press seams in one direction. Sew the B strip to one side edge of one frog square referring to Figure 1; press seam toward B strip.

Figure 1

7. Join six assorted B squares to make a strip; press seams in one direction. Sew this B strip to the top edge of the stitched A-B unit to complete one block, again referring to Figure 1.
8. Repeat steps 6 and 7 to complete eight Frog blocks.

COMPLETING THE NINE-PATCH BLOCKS

1. To complete one Nine-Patch block, join three assorted C squares to make a row; repeat to make three rows. Press seams in one direction.
2. Join the rows to complete the block, alternating seam pressing; press row seams in one direction.
3. Repeat steps 1 and 2 to complete seven Nine-Patch blocks.

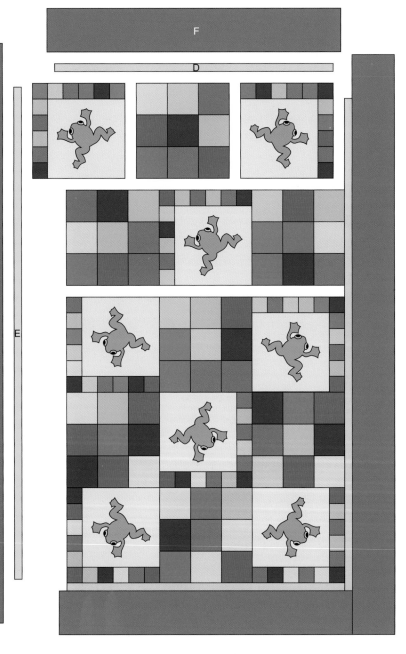

It's Not Easy Being Green
Assembly Diagram 49" x 73"

COMPLETING THE QUILT

1. Join one Nine-Patch block with two Frog blocks to make an X row as shown in Figure 2 and referring to the Assembly Diagram for positioning of Frog blocks in each row; press seams toward Nine-Patch block. Repeat to make three X rows.

2. Join one Frog block with two Nine-Patch blocks to make a Y row, again referring to Figure 2; press seams toward Nine-Patch blocks. Repeat to make two Y rows.

3. Join the X and Y rows to complete the pieced center referring to the Assembly Diagram for positioning of rows; press seams in one direction.

4. Sew a D strip to the top and bottom of the pieced center; press seams toward D strips.

X Row
Make 3

Y Row
Make 2

Figure 2

5. Join the E strips with right sides together on short ends to make one long strip; subcut strip into two 62½" E strips.

6. Sew the E strips to opposite long sides of the pieced center; press seams toward E strips.

7. Sew an F strip to the top and bottom of the pieced center; press seams toward F strips.

8. Join the G strips with right sides together on short ends to make one long strip; subcut strip into two 73½" G strips.

9. Sew the G strips to opposite long sides of the pieced center to complete the top; press seams toward G strips.

10. Create a quilt sandwich referring to Quilting Basics on page 46.

11. Quilt as desired.

12. Bind referring to Quilting Basics on page 46 to finish. ●

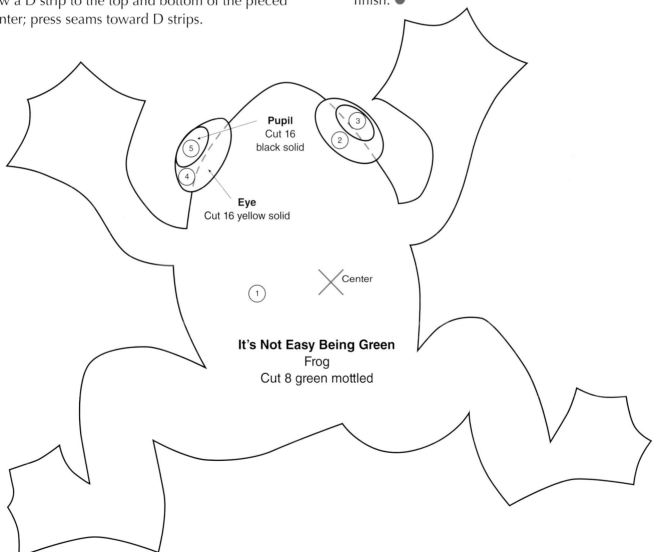

Pupil
Cut 16
black solid

Eye
Cut 16 yellow solid

Center

It's Not Easy Being Green
Frog
Cut 8 green mottled

Little Trip to Bali

Showcase batik scraps in a little bejeweled quilt with the flavors of Bali using Trip Around the World blocks.

Design by Julie Higgins

Skill Level
Intermediate

Finished Size
Quilt Size: 46½" x 46½"
Block Size: 6⅞" x 6⅞" Finished and 6" x 6" Finished
Number of Blocks: 9 and 12

MATERIALS

- ¼ yard total pastel batik scraps
- ½ yard multicolored batik print
- 1 yard total dark batik scraps
- 2¼ yards light mottled batik
- Batting to size
- Backing to size
- Thread
- Dark-color variegated thread
- 1 yard 18"-wide fusible web
- ⅞ yard fabric stabilizer
- Basting spray
- Black fine-tip fabric pen
- Basic sewing tools and supplies

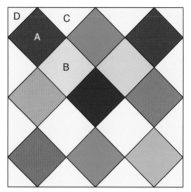

Trip Around the World
6⅞" x 6⅞" Finished Block
Make 9

Elephant
6" x 6" Finished Block
Make 12

CUTTING

Prepare templates for the elephant appliqué motif pieces referring to Quilting Basics on page 46 and using patterns provided. Trace shapes onto the paper side of the fusible web as directed; cut out, leaving a margin around each one. Fuse shapes to wrong side of fabrics as directed. Cut out shapes on traced lines; remove paper backing. Set aside.

From pastel batik scraps:
- Cut 36 (2⅛") B squares.

From multicolored batik print:
- Cut 5 (2¼" by fabric width) binding strips.

From dark batik scraps:
- Cut 137 total 2⅛" A squares.

From light mottled batik:

- Cut 4 (3½" by fabric width) strips.
  Subcut strips into 44 (3½") squares. Cut each square on both diagonals to make 176 C triangles.
- Cut 2 (2" by fabric width) strips.
  Subcut strips into 34 (2") squares. Cut each square in half on 1 diagonal to make 68 D triangles.
- Cut 1 (7⅜" by fabric width) strip.
  Subcut strip into 12 (2⅞") E strips.
- Cut 2 (2¾" x 25⅞") F strips.
- Cut 2 (2¾" x 30⅜") G strips.
- Cut 2 (7" by fabric width) strips.
  Subcut strips into 12 (7") H squares.
- Cut 3 (6½" by fabric width) strips.
  Subcut strips into 8 (8¾") I rectangles and 4 (6½") J squares.

COMPLETING THE TRIP AROUND THE WORLD BLOCKS

1. To complete one Trip Around the World block, join three A and two B squares to make the center diagonal row; add D to each end as shown in Figure 1; press seams toward A.

Figure 1

2. Repeat step 1 with one B and two A squares, adding C to each end to make a side row as shown in Figure 2; press seams toward A. Repeat to make a second side row.

Figure 2

3. Sew C to two opposite sides and D to one side of A to complete a corner unit as shown in Figure 3; repeat to make two corner units.

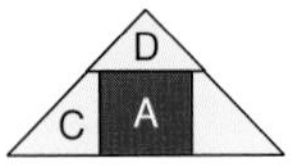

Figure 3

4. Sew the side rows to the center diagonal row as shown in Figure 4; press seams away from the center diagonal row.

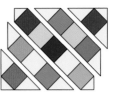

Figure 4

5. Sew a corner unit to each side row, again referring to Figure 4, to complete one Trip Around the World block; press seams toward corner units.

6. Repeat steps 1–5 to complete nine Trip Around the World Blocks.

COMPLETING THE ELEPHANT BLOCKS

1. Fold each H square in half on the vertical and horizontal and crease to mark the centers.
2. Center and fuse an elephant motif on each H square with pieces fused in numerical order.
3. Cut fabric stabilizer into 12 (6") squares. Spray-baste a square of stabilizer to the wrong side of each H square.
4. Machine zigzag-stitch around each appliqué shape using a dark-color variegated thread in the top of the machine and all-purpose thread to match H in the bobbin; remove fabric stabilizer when stitching is complete.
5. Use the black fine-tip fabric pen to add an eye circle to each elephant referring to elephant motif for size and positioning.
6. Trim block to 6½" x 6½", centering elephant motifs, to complete 12 Elephant blocks.

COMPLETING THE TOP

1. Join three Trip Around the World blocks with two E strips to make a block row; press seams toward E strips. Repeat to make three block rows.
2. Sew D to each side of A to make an A-D unit as shown in Figure 5; press seams toward D. Repeat to make four A-D units.

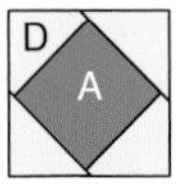

Figure 5

3. Join three E strips with two A-D units to make a sashing row as shown in Figure 6; press seams toward E strips. Repeat to make two sashing strips.

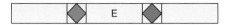

Figure 6

4. Join the block rows with the sashing rows to complete the pieced center; press seams toward the sashing rows.
5. Sew F strips to opposite sides and G strips to the top and bottom of the pieced center; press seams toward F and G strips.
6. Sew C to opposite sides of A to make an A-C unit as shown in Figure 7; press seams toward C. Repeat to make 48 A-C units.

Figure 7

7. Join 11 A-C units to make a side strip as shown in Figure 8; press seams in one direction. Repeat to make two side strips.

Figure 8

8. Repeat step 7 with 13 A-C units to make a top and bottom strip; press seams in one direction.
9. Sew C to one side and D to two adjacent sides of A to complete a corner unit as shown in Figure 9; press seams toward C and D. Repeat to make eight corner units.

Figure 9

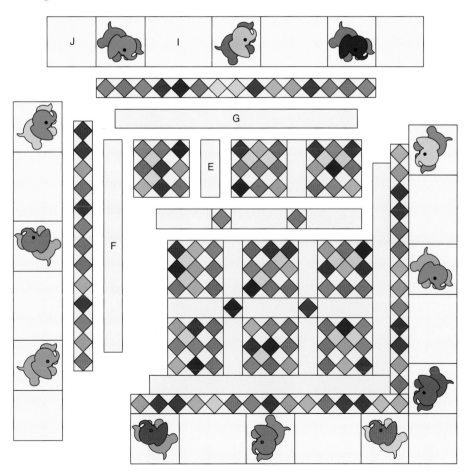

Little Trip to Bali
Assembly Diagram 46¹/₂" x 46¹/₂"

10. Sew a corner unit to each end of each side, top and bottom strip referring to Figure 10 for positioning.

Figure 10

11. Sew a side strip to opposite sides of the pieced center, referring to the Assembly Diagram for positioning of strips; press seams toward F strips. Add the top and bottom strips to the pieced center; press seams toward G strips.

12. Join three Elephant blocks with two I rectangles to make an elephant row referring to the Assembly Diagram for positioning of Elephant blocks; press seams toward I rectangles. Repeat to make four elephant rows.

13. Sew an elephant row to opposite sides of the pieced center, referring to the Placement Diagram for positioning; press seams toward elephant rows.

14. Sew a J square to each end of each remaining elephant row; press seams away from the J squares.

15. Sew the elephant/J rows to the top and bottom of the pieced center to complete the pieced top; press seams toward elephant/J borders.

COMPLETING THE QUILT

1. Create a quilt sandwich referring to Quilting Basics on page 46.
2. Quilt as desired.
3. Bind referring to Quilting Basics on page 46 to finish. ●

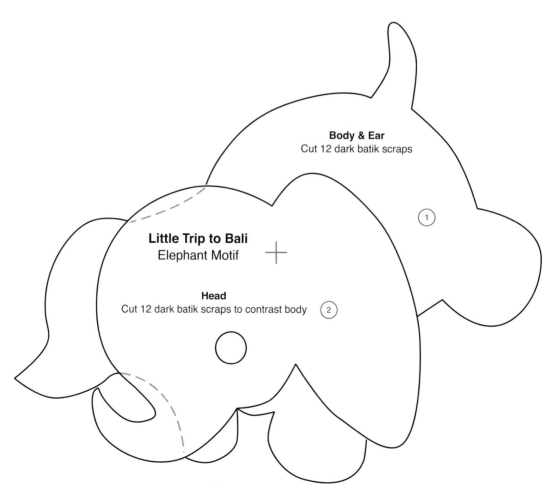

Body & Ear
Cut 12 dark batik scraps

1

Little Trip to Bali
Elephant Motif

Head
Cut 12 dark batik scraps to contrast body   2

Hush-a-Bye

Scrappy squares combine with Snowball blocks to make this old-fashioned–looking baby quilt.

Design by Susan Nelsen of Rasmatazz Designs

Skill Level
Beginner

Finished Size
Quilt Size: 42½" x 42½"
Block Size: 6" x 6" Finished
Number of Blocks: 41

CUTTING

From pink, yellow, green, red and purple reproduction prints:
- Cut 20 (2" x 21") B strips.

From blue reproduction print:
- Cut 20 (2" x 21") A strips.

From red reproduction print:
- Cut 6 (1½" x 21") strips.
  Subcut 80 (1½") C squares.

From yellow reproduction print:
- Cut 1 (9¾" x 42") rectangle.
  Subcut 4 (9¾") squares. Cut each square in half on both diagonals to make 16 E triangles.
- Cut 1 (5⅛" x 42") rectangle.
  Subcut 2 (5⅛") squares. Cut each square in half on 1 diagonal to make 4 F triangles.

From green reproduction print:
- Cut 3 (6½" x 42") rectangles.
  Subcut 16 (6½") D squares.
- Cut 5 (2¼" x 42") binding strips.

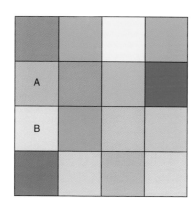

16-Patch
6" x 6" Finished Block
Make 25

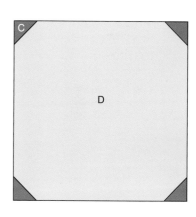

Snowball
6" x 6" Finished Block
Make 16

MATERIALS

- 5 fat eighths or assorted scraps pink, yellow, green, red and purple reproduction prints
- 5 fat eighths or assorted scraps blue reproduction prints
- 1 fat quarter red reproduction print
- ⅝ yard yellow reproduction print
- 1 yard green reproduction print
- Backing to size
- Batting to size
- Thread
- Basic sewing tools and supplies

COMPLETING THE 16-PATCH BLOCKS

1. Sew two each A and B strips together alternately to make an A-B strip set referring to Figure 1; press seams in one direction. Repeat to make 10 strip sets.

Figure 1

2. Subcut the A-B strip sets into (100) 2" A-B units referring again to Figure 1.
3. Join four A-B units, alternating rows, to make one 16-Patch block referring to the block drawing; press seams in one direction. Repeat to make 25 blocks.

COMPLETING THE SNOWBALL BLOCKS

1. Draw a diagonal line from corner to corner on the wrong side of each C square; set aside 16 C squares for side units.
2. Place a C square on each corner of a D square and stitch on the marked lines as shown in Figure 2; trim seam to ¼" and press C to the right side to complete one Snowball block, Repeat to make 16 blocks.

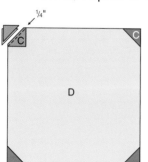

Figure 2

COMPLETING THE QUILT

1. Place a C square on the square corner of an E triangle and stitch on the marked line as shown in Figure 3; trim seam to ¼" and press C to the right side to complete a C-E unit. Repeat to make 16 C-E units.

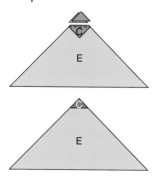

Figure 3

2. Arrange and join the blocks with the C-E units and F triangles in rows as shown in Figure 4; press seams toward the Snowball blocks. Make two each of Rows 1–4 and one of Row 5.
3. Join the pieced rows diagonally, adding F to remaining corners, to complete the pieced top referring to the Assembly Diagram.
4. Create a quilt sandwich referring to Quilting Basics on page 46.
5. Quilt as desired.
6. Bind referring to Quilting Basics on page 46 to finish. ●

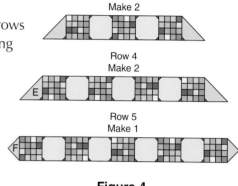

Figure 4

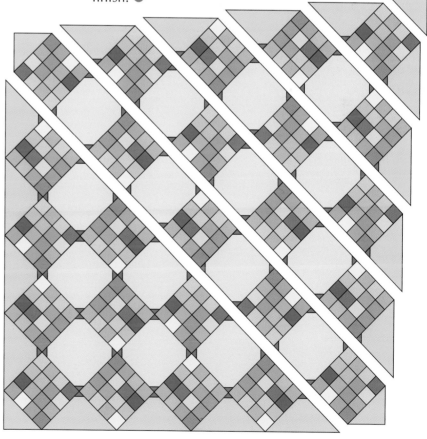

Hush-a-Bye
Assembly Diagram 42½" x 42½"

Diamonds Royale

Whether you use templates or angled rulers, there are only three different shapes in this quick-to-stitch quilt.

Design by Julie Higgins

Project Notes
Piecing the 60-degree diamonds requires sewing with offset seams. Although not really for a beginner, simplified sewing instructions are given. To avoid separate corner and side templates, the quilt is pieced with whole diamond shapes and the excess is trimmed after piecing to square up the edges.

MATERIALS

- 50 (6" x 10") or 1 yard total pastel scraps
- ¼ yard gold solid
- ⅝ yard white solid
- 1⅓ yards blue paisley
- Batting to size
- Backing to size
- Thread
- 60-degree diamond template (optional)
- Basic sewing tools and supplies

Cutting Tip
Use fabric that reads the same from either side to avoid working with mirror images for the C strips.

Skill Level
Intermediate

Finished Size
Quilt Size: 40½" x 50½"

CUTTING

From pastel scraps:
- Prepare A templates using patterns provided; cut A pieces from 6" x 10" rectangles as shown in Figure 1.

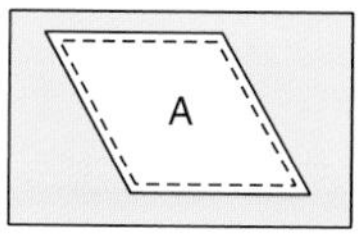

Figure 1

Note: If using yardage, cut seven 4½" by fabric width strips fabric; place template on strip and cut as shown in Figure 2.

Figure 2

From gold solid:

- Cut 3 (1½" by fabric width) strips.
  Prepare B templates using patterns provided and subcut strips into 49 B pieces referring to Figure 3.

Figure 3

- Cut 5 (1¼" by fabric width) E strips.

From white solid:

- Cut 10 (1½" by fabric width) strips.
  Subcut strips into 80 C/CR pieces as shown in Figure 4. *Note: White solid has no right or wrong side, so the template does not have to be reversed to cut the CR pieces because it doesn't matter which side of the piece is used as the right side. If using a fabric with a definite right and wrong side, fold each strip in half with right sides together to make a double-layered strip. Cut using template to make a C and CR piece in one cut as shown in Figure 5.*

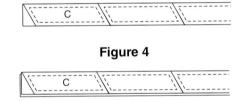

Figure 4

Figure 5

From blue paisley:

- Cut 10 (3" by fabric width) D/F strips.
- Cut 5 (2¼" by fabric width) binding strips.

Cutting Tip

Using a rotary ruler, trim the end of a fabric-width strip at an angle using the 60-degree angle line on the ruler; cut the remainder of the strip every 4½" to make the A pieces without a template as shown in Figure A.

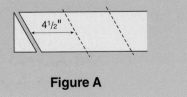

Figure A

COMPLETING THE TOP

1. Join nine A pieces with eight C strips to make a nine-unit row as shown in Figure 6; press seams toward C strips. Repeat to make two nine-unit rows.

Figure 6

2. Repeat step 1 with seven A pieces and six C pieces to make a seven-unit row; press seams toward C strips. Repeat to make two seven-unit rows.

3. Join five A pieces and four C strips to make a five-unit row; press seams toward C strips. Repeat to make two five-unit rows.

4. Join three A pieces and two C strips to make a three-unit row; press seams toward C strips. Repeat to make two three-unit rows.

5. Join eight CR strips with nine B pieces to make an eight-unit sashing row as shown in Figure 7; press seams toward B.

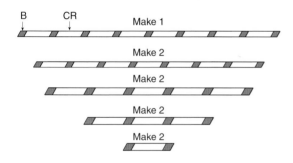

Figure 7

6. Repeat step 5 with seven CR strips and eight B pieces to make an eight-unit sashing row, again referring to Figure 7; press seams toward B. Repeat to make two seven-unit sashing rows.

7. Repeat step 5 to make two each three-unit and five unit sashing rows and two one-unit sashing rows, again referring to Figure 7.

8. Join the sashing rows with the unit rows as shown in Figure 8 to complete the pieced center; press seams toward sashing rows.

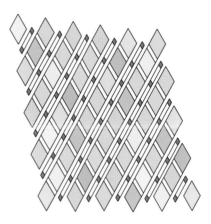

Figure 8

9. Trim excess edges, cutting ¼" below center of outside row of diamonds, as shown in Figure 9. *Note: The size should be approximately 29½" x 40½".*

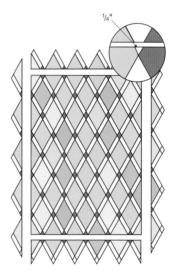

Figure 9

10. Join the D strips on short ends to make one long strip; press seams open. Subcut strip in half to make two long strips.

11. Join the E strips on short ends to make one long strip; press seams open.

12. Sew the E strip between the two D strips to make a D-E-D strip; press seams toward D strips.

13. Subcut the D-E-D strip into two 44" top/bottom strips and two 54" side strips; fold each strip in half and crease to mark the lengthwise center.

14. Fold and crease the pieced top to mark the side and top/bottom centers.

15. Center and pin the top/bottom strips to the top and bottom of the pieced center, leaving excess at each end; stitch in place, stopping stitching ¼" from edges of the pieced top as shown in Figure 10. Press seams toward strips.

Figure 10

16. Repeat step 15 with side strips on opposite long sides of the pieced center; press seams toward strips.

17. To miter corners, lay border strips flat with one on top of the other as shown in Figure 11. Twist the top strip under and away from you, creating a 45-degee angle, aligning the seams of the strips perfectly, again referring to Figure 11; press to form a creased line to use as a guide for stitching.

Figure 11

18. Fold the quilt top in half right sides together on the diagonal; starting at the unstitched seam allowance on the quilt top, stitch along the creased lines, keeping seams of strips perfectly matched as shown in Figure 12.

Figure 12

19. Trim excess to ¼" beyond seam; press seams open to complete one mitered corner as shown in Figure 13. Repeat steps 17–19 to complete all mitered corners.

Figure 13

COMPLETING THE QUILT

1. Complete a quilt sandwich referring to Quilting Basics on page 46.
2. Quilt as desired.
3. Bind referring to Quilting Basics on page 46 to finish. ●

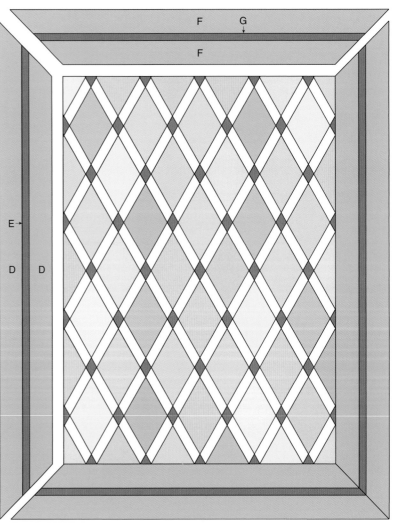

Diamonds Royale Quilt
Assembly Diagram 40½" x 50½"

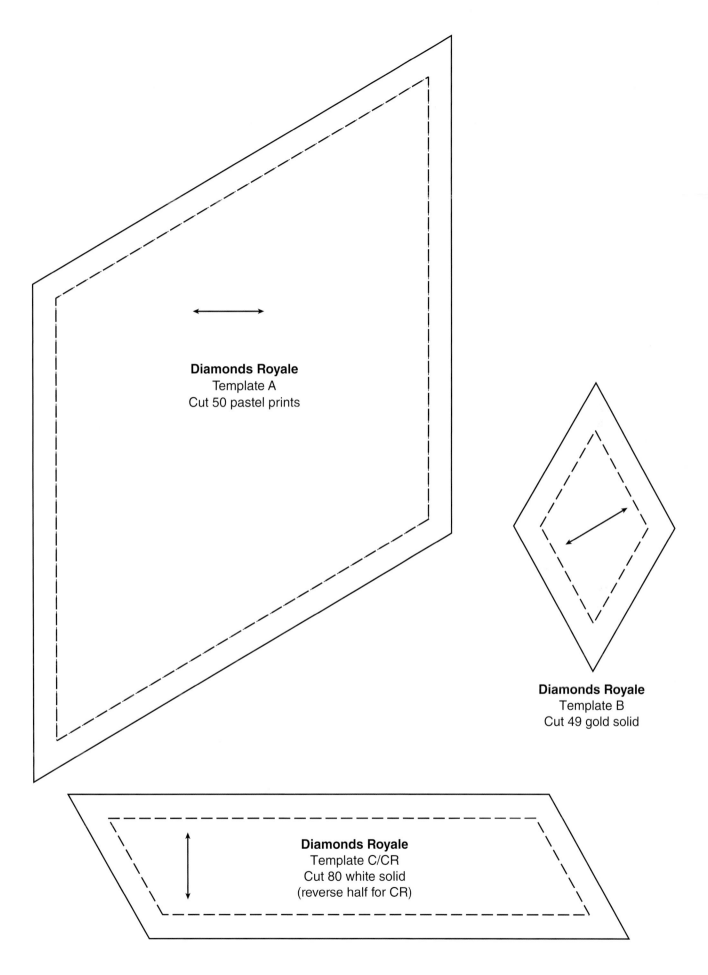

Diamonds Royale
Template A
Cut 50 pastel prints

Diamonds Royale
Template B
Cut 49 gold solid

Diamonds Royale
Template C/CR
Cut 80 white solid
(reverse half for CR)

Pastel Pinwheels

Curved appliqué pieces create pretty pinwheel shapes in this soft-color baby quilt.

Design by Connie Kauffman

Skill Level
Beginner

Finished Size
Quilt Size: 36" x 36"
Block Size: 12" x 12" Finished
Number of Blocks: 9

MATERIALS

- 1 fat quarter each pink, green, purple, blue and yellow tonal
- 3 different fat quarters white tonal
- Backing to size
- Batting to size
- Thread
- Basic sewing tools and supplies

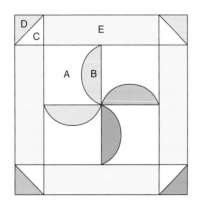

Pastel Pinwheel
12" x 12" Finished Block
Make 9

CUTTING

Prepare template for piece B referring to Quilting Basics on page 46 and using pattern given; cut nine B pieces each from pink, purple, green and blue tonals.

From pink tonal fat quarter:
- Cut 1 (8½" x 21") rectangle.
  Subcut 8 (2½" x 8½") E strips.
- Cut 2 (2⅞") squares.
  Subcut each square on 1 diagonal to make 4 D triangles.

From green tonal fat quarter:
- Cut 1 (8½" x 21") rectangle.
  Subcut 8 (2½" x 8½") E strips.
- Cut 2 (2⅞") squares.
  Subcut each square on 1 diagonal to make 4 D triangles.

From purple tonal fat quarter:
- Cut 1 (8½" x 21") rectangle.
  Subcut 8 (2½" x 8½") E strips.
- Cut 2 (2⅞") squares.
  Subcut each square on 1 diagonal to make 4 D triangles.

From blue tonal fat quarter:
- Cut 1 (8½" x 21") rectangle.
  Subcut 8 (2½" x 8½") E strips.
- Cut 2 (2⅞") squares.
  Subcut each square on 1 diagonal to make 4 D triangles.

From yellow tonal fat quarter:
- Cut 2 (2⅞" x 21") rectangles.
  Subcut 10 (2⅞") squares. Subcut each square on 1 diagonal to make 20 D triangles.
- Cut 2 (2½" x 21") strips.
  Subcut 4 (2½" x 8½") E strips.

From pink, green, purple and blue tonal fat quarter scraps:
- Cut 2¼"-wide strips. Join diagonally on the short ends as shown in Figure 1 to make a 160" binding strip.

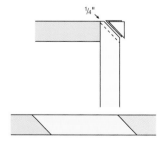

Figure 1

From each white tonal fat quarter:
- Cut 3 (4½" x 21") strips.
  Subcut strips into 12 (4½") A squares each fabric.
- Cut 1 (2⅞" x 21") strip.
  Subcut each strip into 6 (2⅞") squares. Cut each square in half on 1 diagonal to make 12 C triangles each fabric.

COMPLETING THE BLOCKS
1. Turn under the curved edges of each B piece ¼"; baste to hold.
2. To complete one Pastel Pinwheel block, select four each B and D pieces and four same-fabric A and C pieces and four same-fabric E rectangles. **Note:** *Refer to the Assembly Diagram for color placement*

of the D triangles in the block corners. Corners on the outside edges of the quilt are always the yellow/white combination. The center block is bordered with the yellow E rectangles and doesn't use any yellow D triangles at the corners.

3. Align the straight edge of a B piece with one edge of an A square as shown in Figure 2; stitch along straight edge to hold and appliqué curved edge in place to complete one A-B unit. Repeat to make a total of four A-B units.

Figure 2   **Figure 3**

4. Join the four A-B units to complete the block center as shown in Figure 3; press.
5. Sew C to D along the diagonal to make a C-D unit as shown in Figure 4; press seam toward D. Repeat to make four C-D units. **Note:** *Refer to the Assembly Diagram for positioning of colors of the C-D units in the blocks.*

Figure 4

6. Sew an E rectangle to opposite sides of the block center; press seams toward E.
7. Sew a C-D unit to each end of each remaining E rectangle as shown in Figure 5; press seams toward E.

Figure 5

8. Sew the C-D-E units to the remaining sides of the block center as shown in Figure 6 to complete one block; press seams toward E.

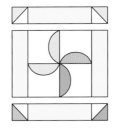

Figure 6

COMPLETING THE QUILT

1. Arrange the pieced blocks in three rows of three blocks each referring to the Assembly Diagram for positioning of blocks.
2. Join blocks in rows; press seams in one direction.
3. Join rows to complete the pieced top.
4. Complete a quilt sandwich referring to Quilting Basics on page 46.
5. Quilt as desired.
6. Bind referring to Quilting Basics on page 46 to finish. ●

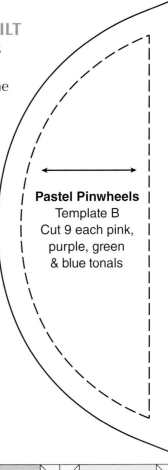

Pastel Pinwheels
Template B
Cut 9 each pink, purple, green & blue tonals

Pastel Pinwheels
Assembly Diagram 36" x 36"

Dots Done Your Way

Polka-dot fabrics and circles create the design in this easy baby quilt.

Design by Joan Ballard

Skill Level
Beginner

Finished Size
Quilt Size: 43½" x 50"
Block Size: 6½" x 6½" Finished and 5½" x 5½" Finished
Number of Blocks: 30 and 4

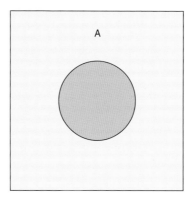

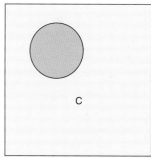

Circle
6½" x 6½" Finished Block
Make 30

Corner
5½" x 5½" Finished Block
Make 4

CUTTING

From each peach, blue and green polka dots:
- Cut 1 (7" by fabric width) strip.
  Subcut 6 (7") A squares.
- Cut 1 (6" by fabric width) strip.
  Subcut a variety of 2"–3½"-wide B strips.

From pink polka dots:
- Cut 1 (7" by fabric width) strip.
  Subcut 6 (7") A squares.
- Cut 1 (6" by fabric width) strip.
  Subcut 2 (6") C squares and a variety of 2"–3½"-wide B strips.

From yellow polka dots:
- Cut 1 (7" by fabric width) strip.
  Subcut 6 (7") A squares.
- Cut 1 (6" by fabric width) strip.
  Subcut 2 (6") C squares and a variety of 2"–3½"-wide B strips.
- Cut 5 (2¼" by fabric width) binding strips.

From fabric stabilizer:
- Cut 50 (4") squares.

PREPARING THE APPLIQUÉ CIRCLES

1. Prepare templates for the circles using the templates provided.
2. Trace circle shapes onto the paper side of the fusible web as directed on each pattern for number to cut; cut out shapes, leaving a margin around each one.
3. Fuse shapes to the wrong side of fabrics as directed on patterns; cut out shapes on traced lines. Remove paper backing.

COMPLETING THE BLOCKS

1. Fold each A square in half vertically and horizontally and crease to mark the centers. Repeat with each large circle.
2. Randomly select an A square and a large circle (not the same fabric); center and fuse the large circle to the A square.
3. Repeat step 2 with all A squares and large circles.
4. Pin a 4" stabilizer square to the wrong side of each fused block. Using a machine blanket stitch and desired color all-purpose thread, stitch around the edge of each circle to complete the blocks; remove fabric stabilizer.
5. Select a small circle and a C square; fuse the circle to the square using random placement. Repeat to make four squares.
6. Repeat step 4 to complete four Corner blocks.

COMPLETING THE QUILT TOP

1. Arrange and join the Circle blocks in six rows of five blocks each, placing colors diagonally from top to bottom as shown in the Assembly Diagram; press seams in adjacent rows in opposite directions.
2. Join the rows to complete the pieced center; press seams in one direction.
3. Join the B strips in peach-yellow-green-pink-blue order along the 6" sides to make a strip at least 145" long; press seams in one direction. Trim strip to make two 39½" E borders and two 33" F borders.
4. Referring to the Assembly Diagram, randomly place and fuse remaining small circles to E and F strips. Repeat step 4 of Completing the Blocks for each circle.

5. Sew E borders to opposite long sides of the pieced center; press seams toward E borders.
6. Sew a Corner block to each end of each F border; press seams toward F borders.
7. Sew the F/Corner borders to the top and bottom of the pieced center to complete the pieced top; press seams toward F/Corner borders.

COMPLETING THE QUILT

1. Press quilt top on both sides; check for proper seam pressing and trim all loose threads.
2. Sandwich batting between the stitched top and the prepared backing piece; pin or baste layers together to hold. Quilt on marked lines and as desired by hand or machine.
3. When quilting is complete, remove pins or basting. Trim batting and backing fabric edges even with raw edges of quilt top.

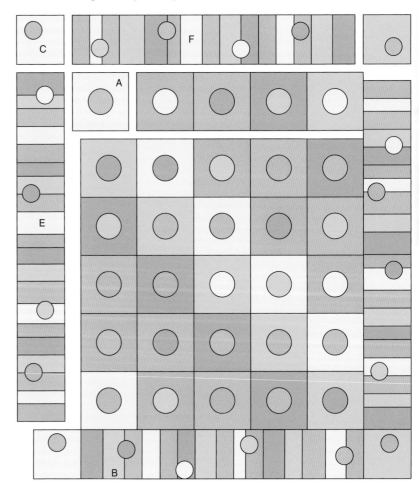

Dots Done Your Way
Assembly Diagram 43½" x 50"

4. Join binding strips on short ends with diagonal seams to make one long strip; trim seams to ¼" and press seams open.

5. Fold the binding strip in half with wrong sides together along length; press.

6. Sew binding to quilt edges, matching raw edges, mitering corners and overlapping ends.

7. Fold binding to the back side and stitch in place to finish. ●

Dots Done Your Way
Small Circle
Cut 4 each polka-dot fabric

Dots Done Your Way
Large Circle
Cut 6 each polka-dot fabric

Grandmother's Diamonds

Use up your reproduction scraps to make this vintage-inspired quilt.

Design by Julie Higgins

Skill Level
Intermediate

Finished Size
Quilt Size: 38½" x 47⅛"

MATERIALS

- ⅝ yard blue solid
- 1 yard cream solid
- 1½ yards total vintage or reproduction print scraps
- Backing to size
- Thin cotton batting to size
- Thread
- Basic sewing tools and supplies

CUTTING

Prepare templates A–D using patterns given and referring to Quilting Basics on page 46; cut as directed on each piece.

From blue solid:

- Cut 2 (1" x 37⅝") E strips.
- Cut 2 (1" x 30") F strips.
- Cut 5 (2¼" by fabric width) binding strips.

From cream solid:

- Cut 2 (5" x 38⅝") G strips.
- Cut 2 (5" x 39") H strips.

COMPLETING THE QUILT

1. Join A pieces in diagonal rows referring to Figure 1 and Sewing Offset Seams on page 44; press seams in adjacent rows in opposite directions.

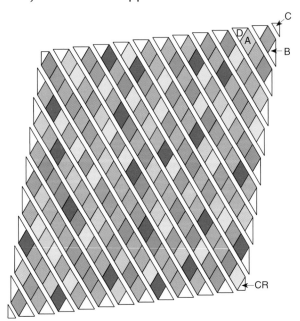

Figure 1

Sewing Offset Seams

If you are new to offsetting seams, it takes a little practice to get to the point where you can match seams on sight.

1. When sewing offset seams, you will have little "ears" protruding at each end of the seam line. Even though these 60-degree diamond shapes look like they would fit together just by aligning edges, it does not work, as shown in Figure A.

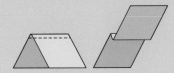

Figure A

2. Align the pieces so that the V formed at the edge of the pieces will intersect exactly with your ¼" seam allowance as shown in Figure B.

Figure B

3. Begin sewing with a ¼" seam allowance as shown in Figure C.

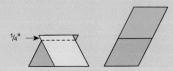

Figure C

4. Be careful when sewing because 60-degree diamonds have bias edges and will stretch easily.

2. Add B, C and D pieces at the ends of rows, again referring to Figure 1; press seams in the same direction as those in the rows to which they are stitched.

3. Join the rows to complete the pieced center; press seams in one direction.

4. Sew E strips to opposite sides and F strips to the top and bottom of the pieced center; press seams toward E and F strips.

5. Sew G strips to opposite sides and H strips to the top and bottom of the pieced center; press seams toward G and H strips.

6. Complete a quilt sandwich referring to Quilting Basics on page 46.

7. Quilt as desired. **Note:** *The wide outside borders are perfect for adding a pretty quilting design.*

8. Bind referring to Quilting Basics on page 46 to finish. ●

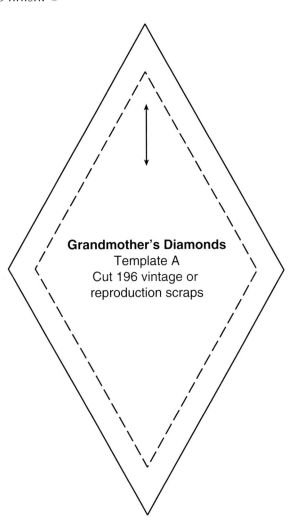

Grandmother's Diamonds
Template A
Cut 196 vintage or
reproduction scraps

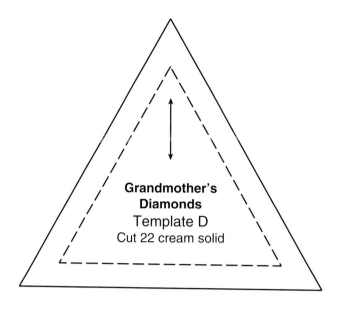

Grandmother's Diamonds
Template D
Cut 22 cream solid

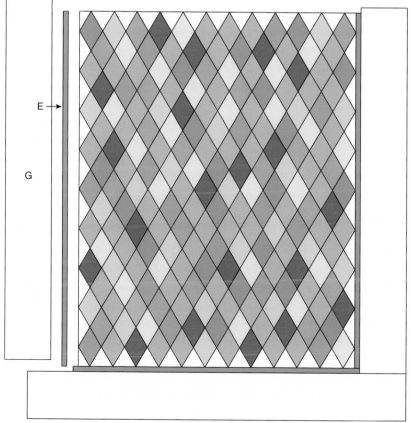

Grandmother's Diamonds
Assembly Diagram 38½" x 47⅛"

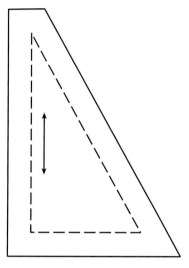

Construction Tip

Apply spray starch to 60-degree diamond fabrics before cutting to help reduce stretching of pieces during the construction process.

Grandmother's Diamonds
Template C
Cut 4 cream solid (reverse half for CR)

Grandmother's Diamonds
Template B
Cut 16 cream solid

Quilting Basics

The following is a reference guide. For more information, consult a comprehensive quilting book.

ALWAYS:

- Read through the entire pattern before you begin your project.
- Purchase quality, 100 percent cotton fabrics.
- When considering prewashing, do so with ALL of the fabrics being used. Generally, prewashing is not required in quilting.
- Use ¼" seam allowance for all stitching unless otherwise instructed.
- Use a short-to-medium stitch length.
- Make sure your seams are accurate.

QUILTING TOOLS & SUPPLIES

- Rotary cutter and mat
- Scissors for paper and fabric
- Nonslip quilting rulers
- Marking tools
- Sewing machine
- Sewing machine feet:
- ¼" seaming foot (for piecing)
- Walking or even-feed foot (for piecing or quilting)
- Darning or free-motion foot (for free-motion quilting)
- Quilting hand-sewing needles
- Straight pins
- Curved safety pins for basting
- Seam ripper
- Iron and ironing surface

BASIC TECHNIQUES
Appliqué
FUSIBLE APPLIQUÉ

All templates are reversed for use with this technique.

1. Trace the instructed number of templates ¼" apart onto the paper side of paper-backed fusible web. Cut apart the templates, leaving a margin around each, and fuse to the wrong side of the fabric following fusible web manufacturer's instructions.
2. Cut the appliqué pieces out on the traced lines, remove paper backing and fuse to the background referring to the appliqué motif given.
3. Finish appliqué raw edges with a straight, satin, blanket, zigzag or blind-hem machine stitch with matching or invisible thread.

TURNED-EDGE APPLIQUÉ

1. Trace the printed reversed templates onto template plastic. Flip the template over and mark as the right side.
2. Position the template, right side up, on the right side of fabric and lightly trace, spacing images ½" apart. Cut apart, leaving a ¼" margin around the traced lines.
3. Clip curves and press edges ¼" to the wrong side around the appliqué shape.
4. Referring to the appliqué motif, pin or baste appliqué shapes to the background.
5. Hand-stitch shapes in place using a blind stitch and thread to match or machine-stitch using a short blind hemstitch and either matching or invisible thread.

Borders

Most patterns give an exact size to cut borders. You may check those sizes by comparing them to the horizontal and vertical center measurements of your quilt top.

STRAIGHT BORDERS

1. Mark the centers of the side borders and quilt top sides.
2. Stitch borders to quilt top sides with right sides together and matching raw edges and center marks using a ¼" seam. Press seams toward borders.
3. Repeat with top and bottom border lengths.

MITERED BORDERS

1. Add at least twice the border width to the border lengths instructed to cut.
2. Center and sew the side borders to the quilt, beginning and ending stitching ¼" from the quilt corner and backstitching (Figure 1). Repeat with the top and bottom borders.

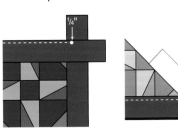

Figure 1   **Figure 2**

3. Fold and pin quilt right sides together at a 45-degree angle on one corner (Figure 2). Place a straightedge along the fold and lightly mark a line across the border ends.

4. Stitch along the line, backstitching to secure. Trim seam to ¼" and press open (Figure 3).

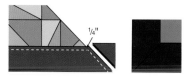

Figure 3

Quilt Backing & Batting

We suggest that you cut your backing and batting 8" larger than the finished quilt-top size. If preparing the backing from standard-width fabrics, remove the selvages and sew two or three lengths together; press seams open. If using 108"-wide fabric, trim to size on the straight grain of the fabric.

Prepare batting the same size as your backing. You can purchase prepackaged sizes or battings by the yard and trim to size.

Quilting

1. Press quilt top on both sides and trim all loose threads.
2. Make a quilt sandwich by layering the backing right side down, batting and quilt top centered right side up on flat surface and smooth out. Pin or baste layers together to hold.
3. Mark quilting design on quilt top and quilt as desired by hand or machine. *Note: If you are sending your quilt to a professional quilter, contact them for specifics about preparing your quilt for quilting.*
4. When quilting is complete, remove pins or basting. Trim batting and backing edges even with raw edges of quilt top.

Binding the Quilt

1. Join binding strips on short ends with diagonal seams to make one long strip; trim seams to ¼" and press seams open (Figure 4).

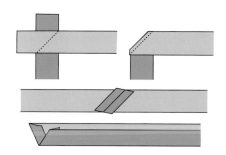

Figure 4

2. Fold 1" of one short end to wrong side and press. Fold the binding strip in half with wrong sides together along length, again referring to Figure 4; press.
3. Starting about 3" from the folded short end, sew binding to quilt top edges, matching raw edges and using a ¼" seam. Stop stitching ¼" from corner and backstitch (Figure 5).

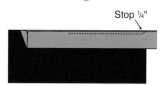

Stop ¼"

Figure 5

4. Fold binding up at a 45-degree angle to seam and then down even with quilt edges, forming a pleat at corner, referring to Figure 6.

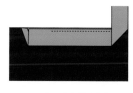

Figure 6

5. Resume stitching from corner edge as shown in Figure 6, down quilt side, backstitching ¼" from next corner. Repeat, mitering all corners, stitching to within 3" of starting point.
6. Trim binding end long enough to tuck inside starting end and complete stitching (Figure 7).

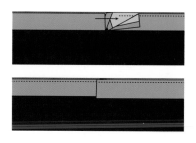

Figure 7

7. Fold binding to quilt back and stitch in place by hand or machine to complete your quilt.

QUILTING TERMS

- **Appliqué:** Adding fabric motifs to a foundation fabric by hand or machine (see Appliqué section of Basic Techniques).
- **Basting:** This temporarily secures layers of quilting materials together with safety pins, thread or a spray adhesive in preparation for quilting the layers.

    Use a long, straight stitch to hand- or machine-stitch one element to another holding the elements in place during construction and usually removed after construction.
- **Batting:** An insulating material made in a variety of fiber contents that is used between the quilt top and back to provide extra warmth and loft.
- **Binding:** A finishing strip of fabric sewn to the outer raw edges of a quilt to cover them.

    Straight-grain binding strips, cut on the crosswise straight grain of the fabric (see Straight & Bias Grain Lines illustration on the next page), are commonly used.

    Bias binding strips are cut at a 45-degree angle to the straight grain of the fabric. They are used when binding is being added to curved edges.
- **Block:** The basic quilting unit that is repeated to complete the quilt's design composition. Blocks can be pieced, appliquéd or solid and are usually square or rectangular in shape.
- **Border:** The frame of a quilt's central design used to visually complete the design and give the eye a place to rest.

- **Fabric Grain:** The fibers that run either parallel (lengthwise grain) or perpendicular (crosswise grain) to the fabric selvage are straight grain.

  Bias is any diagonal line between the lengthwise or crosswise grain. At these angles the fabric is less stable and stretches easily. The true bias of a woven fabric is a 45-degree angle between the lengthwise and crosswise grain lines.

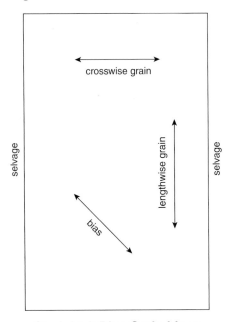

Straight & Bias Grain Lines

- **Mitered Corners:** Matching borders or turning bindings at a 45-degree angle at corners.
- **Patchwork:** A general term for the completed blocks or quilts that are made from smaller shapes sewn together.
- **Pattern:** This may refer to the design of a fabric or to the written instructions for a particular quilt design.
- **Piecing:** The act of sewing smaller pieces and/or units of a block or quilt together.

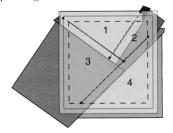

Foundation Piecing

Paper or foundation piecing is sewing fabric to a paper or cloth foundation in a certain order.

String or chain piecing is sewing pieces together in a continuous string without clipping threads between sections.

String or Chain Piecing

Pressing: Pressing is the process of placing the iron on the fabric, lifting it off the fabric and placing it down in another location to flatten seams or crease fabric without sliding the iron across the fabric.

Quilters do not usually use steam when pressing, since it can easily distort fabric shapes.

Generally, seam allowances are pressed toward the darker fabric in quilting so that they do not show through the lighter fabric.

Seams are pressed in opposite directions where seams are being joined to allow seams to butt against each other and to distribute bulk.

Seams are pressed open when multiple seams come together in one place.

If you have a question about pressing direction, consult a comprehensive quilting guide for guidance.

- **Quilt (noun):** A sandwich of two layers of fabric with a third insulating material between them that is then stitched together with the edges covered or bound.
- **Quilt (verb):** Stitching several layers of fabric materials together with a decorative design. Stippling, crosshatch, channel, in-the-ditch, free-motion, allover and meandering are all terms for quilting designs.

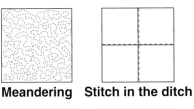

Meandering   **Stitch in the ditch**

       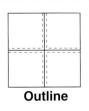

Channel   **Outline**

- **Quilt Sandwich:** A layer of insulating material between a quilt's top and back fabric.
- **Rotary Cutting:** Using a rotary cutting blade and straightedge to cut fabric.
- **Sashing:** Strips of fabric sewn between blocks to separate or set off the designs.
- **Subcut:** A second cutting of rotary-cut strips that makes the basic shapes used in block and quilt construction.
- **Template:** A pattern made from a sturdy material which is then used to cut shapes for patchwork and appliqué quilting.

QUILTING SKILL LEVELS

- **Beginner:** A quilter who has been introduced to the basics of cutting, piecing and assembling a quilt top and is working to master these skills. Someone who has the knowledge of how to sandwich, quilt and bind a quilt, but may not have necessarily accomplished the task yet.
- **Confident Beginner:** A quilter who has pieced and assembled several quilt tops and is comfortable with the process, and is now ready to move on to more challenging techniques and projects using at least two different techniques.
- **Intermediate:** A quilter who is comfortable with most quilting techniques and has a good understanding for design, color and the whole process. A quilter who is experienced in paper piecing, bias piecing and projects involving multiple techniques. Someone who is confident in making fabric selections other than those listed in the pattern.
- **Advanced:** A quilter who is looking for a challenging design. Someone who knows she or he can make any type of quilt. Someone who has the skills to read, comprehend and complete a pattern, and is willing to take on any technique. A quilter who is comfortable in her or his skills and has the ability to select fabric suited to the project. ●